Love Poems

CAROL ANN DUFFY

PICADOR

First published 2010 by Picador

First published in paperback 2010 by Picador
an imprint of Pan Macmillan, a division of Macmillan Publishers Limited
Pan Macmillan, 20 New Wharf Road, London N1 9RR
Basingstoke and Oxford
Associated companies throughout the world
www.panmacmillan.com

ISBN 978-0-330-51272-5

'Correspondents', 'Warming Her Pearls', 'Deportation', 'Miles Away'
from *Selling Manhattan*, first published 1987, Anvil Press Poetry;
'Drunk', 'Valentine', 'Steam', 'Close', 'Adultery', 'The Windows', 'Disgrace', 'Mean Time'
from *Mean Time*, first published 1993, Anvil Press Poetry.

7 9 8 6

A CIP catalogue record for this book is available from
the British Library.

Printed in the UK by CPI Group (UK) Ltd, Croydon, CR0 4YY

This book is sold subject to the condition that it shall not,
by way of trade or otherwise, be lent, re-sold, hired out,
or otherwise circulated without the publisher's prior consent
in any form of binding or cover other than that in which
it is published and without a similar condition including this
condition being imposed on the subsequent purchaser.

Visit www.panmacmillan.com to read more about all our books
and to buy them. You will also find features, author interviews and
news of any author events, and you can sign up for e-newsletters
so that you're always first to hear about our new releases.

Contents

from **The Bees**

from Selling Manhattan

Correspondents

When you come on Thursday, bring me a letter. We have
the language of stuffed birds, teacups. We don't have
the language of bodies. My husband will be here.
I shall inquire after your wife, stirring his cup
with a thin spoon and my hand shall not tremble.
Give me the letter as I take your hat. Mention
the cold weather. My skin burns at the sight of you.

We skim the surface, gossip. I baked this cake and you
eat it. Words come from nowhere, drift off
like the smoke from his pipe. Beneath my dress, my breasts
swell for your lips, belly churns to be stilled
by your brown hands. This secret life is Gulliver,
held down by strings of pleasantries. I ache. Later
your letter flares up in the heat and is gone.

Dearest Beloved, pretend I am with you . . . I read
your dark words and do to myself things
you can only imagine. I hardly know myself.
Your soft, white body in my arms . . . When we part,
you kiss my hand, bow from the waist, all passion
patiently restrained. *Your servant, Ma'am.* Now you write
wild phrases of love. The words blur as I cry out once.

Next time we meet, in drawing-room or garden,
passing our letters cautiously between us, our eyes
fixed carefully on legal love, think of me here
on my marriage-bed an hour after you've left.
I have called your name over and over in my head
at the point your fiction brings me to. I have kissed
your sweet name on the paper as I knelt by the fire.

Warming Her Pearls

Next to my own skin, her pearls. My mistress
bids me wear them, warm them, until evening
when I'll brush her hair. At six, I place them
round her cool, white throat. All day I think of her,

resting in the Yellow Room, contemplating silk
or taffeta, which gown tonight? She fans herself
whilst I work willingly, my slow heat entering
each pearl. Slack on my neck, her rope.

She's beautiful. I dream about her
in my attic bed; picture her dancing
with tall men, puzzled by my faint, persistent scent
beneath her French perfume, her milky stones.

I dust her shoulders with a rabbit's foot,
watch the soft blush seep through her skin
like an indolent sigh. In her looking-glass
my red lips part as though I want to speak.

Full moon. Her carriage brings her home. I see
her every movement in my head. . . . Undressing,,
taking off her jewels, her slim hand reaching
for the case, slipping naked into bed, the way

she always does. . . . And I lie here awake,
knowing the pearls are cooling even now
in the room where my mistress sleeps. All night
I feel their absence and I burn.

Deportation

They have not been kind here. Now I must leave,
the words I've learned for supplication,
gratitude, will go unused. Love is a look
in the eyes in any language, but not here,
not this year. They have not been welcoming.

I used to think the world was where we lived
in space, one country shining in big dark.
I saw a photograph when I was small.

Now I am *Alien*. Where I come from there are few jobs,
the young are sullen and do not dream. My lover
bears our child and I was to work here, find
a home. In twenty years we would say This is you
when you were a baby, when the plum tree was a shoot . . .

We will tire each other out, making our homes
in one another's arms. We are not strong enough.

They are polite, recite official jargon endlessly.
Form F. Room 12. Box 6. I have felt less small
below mountains disappearing into cloud
than entering the Building of Exile. Hearse taxis
crawl the drizzling streets towards the terminal.

I am no one special. An ocean parts me from my love.

Go back. She will embrace me, ask what it was like.
Return. One thing – there was a space to write
the colour of her eyes. They have an apple here,
a bitter-sweet, which matches them exactly. Dearest,
without you I am nowhere. It was cold.

Miles Away

I want you and you are not here. I pause
in this garden, breathing the colour thought is
before language into still air. Even your name
is a pale ghost and, though I exhale it again
and again, it will not stay with me. Tonight
I make you up, imagine you, your movements clearer
than the words I have you say you said before.

Wherever you are now, inside my head you fix me
with a look, standing here while cool late light
dissolves into the earth. I have got your mouth wrong,
but still it smiles. I hold you closer, miles away,
inventing love, until the calls of nightjars
interrupt and turn what was to come, was certain,
into memory. The stars are filming us for no one.

from The Other Country

Who Loves You

I worry about you travelling in those mystical machines.
Every day people fall from the clouds, dead.
Breathe in and out and in and out easy.
Safety, safely, safe home.

Your photograph is in the fridge, smiles when the light comes on.
All the time people are burnt in the public places.
Rest where the cool trees drop to a gentle shade.
Safety, safely, safe home.

Don't lie down on the sands where the hole in the sky is.
Too many people being gnawed to shreds.
Send me your voice however it comes across oceans.
Safety, safely, safe home.

The loveless men and homeless boys are out there and angry.
Nightly people end their lives in the shortcut.
Walk in the light, steadily hurry towards me.
Safety, safely, safe home. (Who loves you?)
Safety, safely, safe home.

Girlfriends

derived from Verlaine

That hot September night, we slept in a single bed,
naked, and on our frail bodies the sweat
cooled and renewed itself. I reached out my arms
and you, hands on my breasts, kissed me. Evening of amber.

Our nightgowns lay on the floor where you fell to your knees
and became ferocious, pressed your head to my stomach,
your mouth to the red gold, the pink shadows; except
I did not see it like this at the time, but arched

my back and squeezed water from the sultry air
with my fists. Also I remember hearing, clearly
but distantly, a siren some streets away – *de*

da de da de da – which mingled with my own
absurd cries, so that I looked up, even then,
to see my fingers counting themselves, dancing.

Words, Wide Night

Somewhere on the other side of this wide night
and the distance between us, I am thinking of you.
The room is turning slowly away from the moon.

This is pleasurable. Or shall I cross that out and say
it is sad? In one of the tenses I singing
an impossible song of desire that you cannot hear.

La lala la. See? I close my eyes and imagine
the dark hills I would have to cross
to reach you. For I am in love with you and this

is what it is like or what it is like in words.

The *Darling* Letters

Some keep them in shoeboxes away from the light,
sore memories blinking out as the lid lifts,
their own recklessness written all over them. *My own . . .*
Private jokes, no longer comprehended, pull their punchlines,
fall flat in the gaps between endearments. *What
are you wearing?*

                    Don't ever change.
They start with *Darling*; end in recriminations,
absence, sense of loss. Even now, the fist's bud flowers
into trembling, the fingers trace each line and see
the future then. *Always . . .* Nobody burns them,
the *Darling* letters, stiff in their cardboard coffins.

Babykins . . . We all had strange names
which make us blush, as though we'd murdered
someone under an alias, long ago. *I'll die
without you. Die.* Once in a while, alone,
we take them out to read again, the heart thudding
like a spade on buried bones.

from New Selected Poems

To the Unknown Lover

Horrifying, the very thought of you,
whoever you are,
future knife to my scar,
stay where you are.

Be handsome, beautiful, drop-dead
gorgeous, keep away.
Read my lips.
No way. OK?

This old heart of mine's
an empty purse.
These ears are closed.
Don't phone, want dinner,

make things worse.
Your little quirks?
Your wee endearing ways?
What makes you you, all that?

Stuff it, mount it, hang it
on the wall, sell tickets,
I won't come. Get back. Get lost.
Get real. Get a life. Keep schtum.

And just, you must, remember this –
there'll be no kiss, no clinch,
no smoochy dance, no true romance.
You are *Anonymous*. You're *Who?*

Here's not looking, kid, at you.

from Mean Time

Drunk

Suddenly the rain is hilarious.
The moon wobbles in the dusk.

What a laugh. Unseen frogs
belch in the damp grass.

The strange perfumes of darkening trees.
Cheap red wine

and the whole world a mouth.
Give me a double, a kiss.

Valentine

Not a red rose or a satin heart.

I give you an onion.
It is a moon wrapped in brown paper.
It promises light
like the careful undressing of love.

Here.
It will blind you with tears
like a lover.
It will make your reflection
a wobbling photo of grief.

I am trying to be truthful.

Not a cute card or a kissogram.

I give you an onion.
Its fierce kiss will stay on your lips,
possessive and faithful
as we are,
for as long as we are.

Take it.
Its platinum loops shrink to a wedding-ring,
if you like.
Lethal.
Its scent will cling to your fingers,
cling to your knife.

Steam

Not long ago so far, a lover and I
in a room of steam –

a sly, thirsty, silvery word – lay down,
opposite ends, and vanished.

Quite recently, if one of us sat up,
or stood, or stretched, naked,

a nude pose in soft pencil
behind tissue paper

appeared, rubbed itself out, slow,
with a smoky cloth.

Say a matter of months. This hand reaching
through the steam

to touch the real thing, shockingly there,
not a ghost at all.

Close

Lock the door. In the dark journey of our night,
two childhoods stand in the corner of the bedroom
watching the way we take each other to bits
to stare at our heart. I hear a story
told in sleep in a lost accent. You know the words.

Undress. A suitcase crammed with secrets
bursts in the wardrobe at the foot of the bed.
Dress again. Undress. You have me like a drawing,
erased, coloured in, untitled, signed by your tongue.
The name of a country written in red on my palm,

unreadable. I tell myself where I live now,
but you move in close till I shake, homeless,
further than that. A coin falls from the bedside table,
spinning its heads and tails. How the hell
can I win. How can I lose. Tell me again.

Love won't give in. It makes a hired room tremble
with the pity of bells, a cigarette smoke itself
next to a full glass of wine, time ache
into space, space, wants no more talk. Now
it has me where I want me, now you, you do.

Put out the light. Years stand outside on the street
looking up to an open window, black as our mouth
which utters its tuneless song. The ghosts of ourselves,
behind and before us, throng in a mirror, blind,
laughing and weeping. They know who we are.

Adultery

Wear dark glasses in the rain.
Regard what was unhurt
as though through a bruise.
Guilt. A sick, green tint.

New gloves, money tucked in the palms,
the handshake crackles. Hands
can do many things. Phone.
Open the wine. Wash themselves. Now

you are naked under your clothes all day,
slim with deceit. Only the once
brings you alone to your knees,
miming, more, more, older and sadder,

creative. Suck a lie with a hole in it
on the way home from a lethal, thrilling night
up against a wall, faster. Language
unpeels to a lost cry. You're a bastard.

Do it do it do it. Sweet darkness
in the afternoon; a voice in your ear
telling you how you are wanted,
which way, now. A telltale clock

wiping the hours from its face, your face
on a white sheet, gasping, radiant, yes.
Pay for it in cash, fiction, cab-fares back
to the life which crumbles like a wedding-cake.

Paranoia for lunch; too much
to drink, as a hand on your thigh
tilts the restaurant. You know all about love,
don't you. Turn on your beautiful eyes

for a stranger who's dynamite in bed, again
and again; a slow replay in the kitchen
where the slicing of innocent onions
scalds you to tears. Then, selfish autobiographical sleep

in a marital bed, the tarnished spoon of your body
stirring betrayal, your heart over-ripe at the core.
You're an expert, darling; your flowers
dumb and explicit on nobody's birthday.

So write the script – illness and debt,
a ring thrown away in a garden
no moon can heal, your own words
commuting to bile in your mouth, terror –

and all for the same thing twice. And all
for the same thing twice. You did it.
What. Didn't you. Fuck. Fuck. No. That was
the wrong verb. This is only an abstract noun.

The Windows

How do you earn a life going on
behind yellow windows, writing at night
the Latin names of plants for a garden,
opening the front door to a wet dog?

Those you love forgive you, clearly,
with steaming casseroles and red wine.
It's the same film down all the suburban streets,
It's A Wonderful Life. How do you learn it?

What you hear – the doorbell's familiar chime.
What you touch – the clean, warm towels.
What you see what you smell what you taste
all tangible to the stranger passing your gate.

There you are again, in a room where those early hyacinths
surely sweeten the air, and the right words wait
in the dictionaries, on the tip of the tongue you touch
in a kiss, drawing your crimson curtains now

against dark hours. And again, in a kitchen,
the window ajar, sometimes the sound of your radio
or the scent of your food, and a cat in your arms,
a child in your arms, a lover. Such vivid flowers.

Disgrace

But one day we woke to disgrace; our house
a coldness of rooms, each nursing
a thickening cyst of dust and gloom.
We had not been home in our hearts for months.

And how our words changed. Dead flies in a web.
How they stiffened and blackened. Cherished italics
suddenly sour on our tongues, obscenities
spraying themselves on the wall in my head.

Woke to your clothes like a corpse on the floor,
the small deaths of lightbulbs pining all day
in my ears, their echoes audible tears;
nothing we would not do to make it worse

and worse. Into the night with the wrong language,
waving and pointing, the shadows of hands
huge in the bedroom. Dreamed of a naked crawl
from a dead place over the other; both of us. Woke.

Woke to the absence of grace; the still-life
of a meal, untouched, wine-bottle, empty, ashtray,
full. In our sullen kitchen, the fridge
hardened its cool heart, selfish as art, hummed.

To a bowl of apples rotten to the core. Lame shoes
empty in the hall where our voices asked
for a message after the tone, the telephone
pressing its ear to distant, invisible lips.

And our garden bowing its head, vulnerable flowers
unseen in the dusk as we shouted in silhouette.
Woke to the screaming alarm, the banging door,
the house-plants trembling in their brittle soil. Total

disgrace. Up in the dark to stand at the window,
counting the years to arrive there, faithless,
unpenitent. Woke to the meaningless stars, you
and me both, lost. Inconsolable vowels from the next room.

Mean Time

The clocks slid back an hour
and stole light from my life
as I walked through the wrong part of town,
mourning our love.

And, of course, unmendable rain
fell to the bleak streets
where I felt my heart gnaw
at all our mistakes.

If the darkening sky could lift
more than one hour from this day
there are words I would never have said
nor have heard you say.

But we will be dead, as we know,
beyond all light.
These are the shortened days
and the endless nights.

from New Selected Poems

Twinned

I have been wined and dined
in the town with which this one is twinned.
The people were kind, I found.

I have walked hand in hand,
scraped two names and a heart with a stick on the sand
in the town with which this one is twinned,
become over-soon over-fond.

And stayed in my room when it rained,
hearing the wind,
with love love love on my mind,
in the town with which this one is twinned,
and pined.

So one day I left it behind –
what little I owned,
whatever I'd gained;
and composed a letter to send,
in the town with which this one is twinned,
to a practical friend.

Then went to see what I'd find
in a different land
where the life, so they said, was grand;
for I had nothing particular planned,
had only the future once read from the palm of my hand
in the town with which this one is twinned,
and a broken heart for somebody somewhere to mend.

Uncollected

Twin

And another thing, don't say we're the same
when you're unwell and I play nurse, pour chamomile
tea, poor baby. Or you put down a winning word
that I don't know and I have to look it up
in our OED. I love our eyes, our lips,
but not that dark red gloss and not
when you put it on to go out and smile at the friend.

Identical. But not when you haven't pierced
your ears. Not when you start to bleed
two days before, or you pull on jeans
when I want us to wear a skirt. I brush
your hair in the mirror and make you watch;
the mole on your shoulder fuzzy under my thumb.
I feel myself coming down with the dose you had,

so put me in my twin bed and spoon our favourite soup
into my mouth. Turn off the light. We lie on our backs
in the dark; and when I look over, your profile
does it to me again. Every time. I whisper
the words till you come across, barefooted, shy,
and say exactly the same ones back in my ear, same
ones back in your ear. Your synonymous breath.

from The World's Wife

Delilah

Teach me, he said –
we were lying in bed –
how to care.
I nibbled the purse of his ear.
What do you mean? Tell me more.
He sat up and reached for his beer.

I can rip out the roar
from the throat of a tiger,
or gargle with fire,
or sleep one whole night in the Minotaur's lair,
or flay the bellowing fur
from a bear,
all for a dare.
There's nothing I fear.
Put your hand here –

he guided my fingers over the scar
over his heart,
a four-medal wound from the war –
but I cannot be gentle, or loving, or tender.
I have to be strong.
What is the cure?

He fucked me again
until he was sore,
then we both took a shower.
Then he lay with his head on my lap
for a darkening hour;
his voice, for a change, a soft burr
I could just about hear.
And, yes, I was sure
that he wanted to change,
my warrior.

I was there.

So when I felt him soften and sleep,
when he started, as usual, to snore,
I let him slip and slide and sprawl, handsome and huge,
on the floor.
And before I fetched and sharpened my scissors –
snipping first at the black and biblical air –
I fastened the chain to the door.

That's the how and the why and the where.

Then with deliberate, passionate hands
I cut every lock of his hair.

Anne Hathaway

'Item I gyve unto my wief my second best bed . . .'
(from Shakespeare's will)

The bed we loved in was a spinning world
of forests, castles, torchlight, clifftops, seas
where he would dive for pearls. My lover's words
were shooting stars which fell to earth as kisses
on these lips; my body now a softer rhyme
to his, now echo, assonance; his touch
a verb dancing in the centre of a noun.
Some nights, I dreamed he'd written me, the bed
a page beneath his writer's hands. Romance
and drama played by touch, by scent, by taste.
In the other bed, the best, our guests dozed on,
dribbling their prose. My living laughing love –
I hold him in the casket of my widow's head
as he held me upon that next best bed.

Mrs Lazarus

I had grieved. I had wept for a night and a day
over my loss, ripped the cloth I was married in
from my breasts, howled, shrieked, clawed
at the burial stones till my hands bled, retched
his name over and over again, dead, dead.

Gone home. Gutted the place. Slept in a single cot,
widow, one empty glove, white femur
in the dust, half. Stuffed dark suits
into black bags, shuffled in a dead man's shoes,
noosed the double knot of a tie round my bare neck,

gaunt nun in the mirror; touching herself. I learnt
the Stations of Bereavement, the icon of my face
in each bleak frame; but all those months
he was going away from me, dwindling
to the shrunk size of a snapshot, going,

going. Till his name was no longer a certain spell
for his face. The last hair on his head
floated out from a book. His scent went from the house.
The will was read. See, he was vanishing
to the small zero held by the gold of my ring.

Then he was gone. Then he was legend, language;
my arm on the arm of the schoolteacher – the shock
of a man's strength under the sleeve of his coat –
along the hedgerows. But I was faithful
for as long as it took. Until he was memory.

So I could stand that evening in the field
in a shawl of fine air, healed, able
to watch the edge of the moon occur to the sky
and a hare thump from a hedge; then notice
the village men running towards me, shouting,

behind them the women and children, barking dogs,
and I knew. I knew by the sly light
on the blacksmith's face, the shrill eyes
of the barmaid, the sudden hands bearing me
into the hot tang of the crowd parting before me.

He lived. I saw the horror on his face.
I heard his mother's crazy song. I breathed
his stench; my bridegroom in his rotting shroud,
moist and dishevelled from the grave's slack chew,
croaking his cuckold name, disinherited, out of his time.

from Feminine Gospels

White Writing

No vows written to wed you,
I write them white,
my lips on yours,
light in the soft hours of our married years.

No prayers written to bless you,
I write them white,
your soul a flame,
bright in the window of your maiden name.

No laws written to guard you,
I write them white,
your hand in mine,
palm against palm, lifeline, heartline.

No rules written to guide you,
I write them white,
words on the wind,
traced with a stick where we walk on the sand.

No news written to tell you,
I write it white,
foam on a wave
as we lift up our skirts in the sea, wade,

see last gold sun behind clouds,
inked water in moonlight.
No poems written to praise you,
I write them white.

North-West

However it is we return to the water's edge
where the ferry grieves down by the Pier Head,
we do what we always did and get on board.
The city drifts out of reach. A huge silvery bird,
a kiss on the lip of the wind, follows our ship.
This is where we were young, the place no map
or heritage guide can reveal. Only an X on a wave
marks the spot, the flowers of litter, a grave
for our ruined loves, unborn children, ghosts.
We look back at the skyline wondering what we lost
in the hidden streets, in the rented rooms,
no more than punters now in a tourist boom.
Above our heads the gulls cry *yeah yeah yeah*.
Frets of light on the river. Tearful air.

from Rapture

Text

I tend the mobile now
like an injured bird.

We text, text, text
our significant words.

I re-read your first,
your second, your third,

look for your small *xx*,
feeling absurd.

The codes we send
arrive with a broken chord.

I try to picture your hands,
their image is blurred.

Nothing my thumbs press
will ever be heard.

Hour

Love's time's beggar, but even a single hour,
bright as a dropped coin, makes love rich.
We find an hour together, spend it not on flowers
or wine, but the whole of the summer sky and a grass ditch.

For thousands of seconds we kiss; your hair
like treasure on the ground; the Midas light
turning your limbs to gold. Time slows, for here
we are millionaires, backhanding the night

so nothing dark will end our shining hour,
no jewel hold a candle to the cuckoo spit
hung from the blade of grass at your ear,
no chandelier or spotlight see you better lit

than here. Now. Time hates love, wants love poor,
but love spins gold, gold, gold from straw.

If I Was Dead

If I was dead,
and my bones adrift
like dropped oars
in the deep, turning earth;

or drowned,
and my skull
a listening shell
on the dark ocean bed;

if I was dead,
and my heart
soft mulch
for a red, red rose;

or burned,
and my body
a fistful of grit, thrown
in the face of the wind;

if I was dead,
and my eyes,
blind at the roots of flowers,
wept into nothing,

I swear your love
would raise me
out of my grave,
in my flesh and blood,

like Lazarus;
hungry for this,
and this, and this,
your living kiss.

Tea

I like pouring your tea, lifting
the heavy pot, and tipping it up,
so the fragrant liquid steams in your china cup.

Or when you're away, or at work,
I like to think of your cupped hands as you sip,
as you sip, of the faint half-smile of your lips.

I like the questions – sugar? milk? –
and the answers I don't know by heart, yet,
for I see your soul in your eyes, and I forget.

Jasmine, Gunpowder, Assam, Earl Grey, Ceylon,
I love tea's names. Which tea would you like? I say,
but it's any tea, for you, please, any time of day,

as the women harvest the slopes,
for the sweetest leaves, on Mount Wu-Yi,
and I am your lover, smitten, straining your tea.

Syntax

I want to call you thou, the sound
of the shape of the start
of a kiss – like this, thou –
and to say, after, I love,
thou, I love, thou I love, not
I love you.

Because I so do –
as we say now – I want to say
thee, I adore, I adore thee,
and to know in my lips
the syntax of love resides,
and to gaze in thine eyes.

Love's language starts, stops, starts;
the right words flowing or clotting in the heart.

The Love Poem

Till love exhausts itself, longs
for the sleep of words –

              my mistress' eyes
to lie on a white sheet, at rest
in the language –

     let me count the ways –
or shrink to a phrase like an epitaph –

                  come live

with me –
or fall from its own high cloud as syllables
in a pool of verse –

          one hour with thee.

Till love gives in and speaks
in the whisper of art –

        dear heart,
how like you this? –
love's lips pursed to quotation marks
kissing a line –

        look in thy heart

and write –
love's light fading, darkening,
black as ink on a page –

            there is a garden
in her face.

Till love is all in the mind –

                    O my America

my new-found land –
or all in the pen
in the writer's hand –

                     behold, thou art fair –
not there, except in a poem,
known by heart like a prayer,
both near and far,
near and far –

              the desire of the moth
for the star.

from The Bees

(forthcoming 2011)

Sung

Now only words in a rhyme,
no more than a name
on a stone,
and that well overgrown –
MAR– –ORIS––;

and wind though a ruined croft,
the door an appalled mouth,
the window's eye put out;

hours and wishes and trysts
less than the shadows of clouds on grass,
ghosts that did dance, did dance . . .

and those who would gladly die for love lang deid –
a skull for a bonnie head –
and love itself a metaphor, rose, red.

At Ballynahinch

I lay by the river at Ballynahinch
and saw the light hurl down
like hammers flung by the sun
to light-stun me, batter
the water to pewter,
everything dream or myth,
my own death further upstream;
the sleeping breath now – by my side
in our wounded sprawl – of the one
who did not love me at all,
who had never loved me, no,
who would never love me, I knew,
down by the star-thrashed river at Ballynahinch,
at Ballynahinch, at Ballynahinch, at Ballynahinch.

Leda

Obsessed by faithfulness,
                            I went to the river
where the swans swam in their pairs and saw how a heart
formed in the air as they touched, partnered forever.
Under the weeping trees a lone swan swam apart.

I knelt like a bride as bees prayed in the clover
and he rose, huge, an angel, out of the water,
to cover me, my beaked, feathered, webbed, winged lover;
a chaos of passion beating the fair day whiter.

My hands, frantic to hold him, felt flight, force, friction,
his weird beautiful form rising and falling above –
the waxy intimate creak –
                            as though he might fly,
turn all my unborn children into fiction.
I knew their names that instant, pierced by love
and by the song the swans sing when they die.

New Vows

From this day forth to unhold,
to see the nothing in ringed gold,
uncare for you when you are old.

New vows you make me swear to keep –
not ever wake with you, or sleep,
or your body with my own worship;

this living hand slipped from your glove,
these lips sip never from our loving cup,
I may not cherish, kiss; unhave, unlove . . .

And all my worthless worldly goods to unendow . . .
And who here present upon whom I call . . .